Connecting
with
Students

Allen N. Mendler

Association for Supervision and Curriculum Development
Alexandria, VA USA

Association for Supervision and Curriculum Development
1703 N. Beauregard St. • Alexandria, VA 22311-1714 USA
Telephone: 1-800-933-2723 or 703-578-9600 • Fax: 703-575-5400
Web site: http://www.ascd.org • E-mail: member@ascd.org

Printed in the United States of America.

ASCD Product No. 101236

ASCD member price: $11.95   nonmember price: $13.95

s11/2001

Library of Congress Cataloging-in-Publication Data
Mendler, Allen N.
  Connecting with students / Allen N. Mendler.
    p. cm.
Includes bibliographical references.
"ASCD product no. 101236"—T.p. verso.
  ISBN 0-87120-573-4 (alk. paper)
  1. Teacher-student relationships. 2. Classroom management. I. Title.

  LB1033 .M415 2001
  371.102'3—dc21
                                          2001005300

07 06 05 04 03 02   10 9 8 7 6 5 4 3 2

Connecting
with
Students

*To the memory of
the innocent victims of school
violence and their families:*

Your terrible loss inspires me to help

make and keep our schools safe places. Too often

it is disconnected, withdrawn, and quietly angry

young people who wreak havoc and visit

tragedy upon what must become secure halls

of learning. I hope that the practical strategies in this

book will assist caring educators to create and

maintain a daily climate that will help each student

find positive ways to feel connected,

valued, and special.

Acknowledgments ~

I wish to thank the many educators who attend my workshops and seminars. At each seminar, I ask colleagues to share practical, concrete, user-friendly strategies that have worked to enhance their relationships with difficult students. I am therefore privileged to learn from educators each day and to pass along the learning to others. Unfortunately, because of time constraints and large numbers of people to thank, I am not always able to remember who shared each strategy. My sincerest gratitude to those of you who I am unable to specifically acknowledge but to whom I am deeply appreciative for sharing so many wonderful ideas that I can pass along to others.

Special thanks to Steph Selice, my acquisitions editor, and Nancy Modrak, director of publishing at ASCD, for their enthusiasm, support, and suggestions. As always, my appreciation to Rick Curwin for his unending stream of creative ideas that stimulates my thinking, and Tammy Rowland, my program manager at Discipline Associates, who does an excellent job working to keep my professional life in balance. I want to thank my wife and outstanding special educator, Barbara Mendler, for her input, feedback, and

unending support. Finally, my heartfelt appreciation
to the many awesome educators I meet every day who
are committed to making school a welcoming place
for all students.

● ● ●

Take Me by the Hand

I was sitting on the couch flipping through the
     stations,
When something came on that affected the nation.
Two boys' actions caused a lot of grief in a little ole
     town,
The story hit hard and brought spirits down.
It was an act of violence that didn't make sense
Now it's weighing on our conscience.
I don't know where I'm going, don't know where
     I'm bound,

Everywhere I look it seems to follow me
But in my mind it's plain to see
The actions of a few can change the world's views,
For better or worse it starts with us of course.
We can stop the violence and stop the pain
Sharing our love is not the same.
Person to person making the connection
We need each other for protection.
                    —Tiffany Caputo, 7th grade student

(A portion of a poem written around the time of
the Columbine High School shootings. Reproduced
by permission.)

Introduction ~

In the aftermath of horrific, high-profile acts of school violence visited upon innocent children by distressed peers obsessed with death and violence, many people have blamed our schools. They point to the depersonalized nature of large, cavernous, increasingly overcrowded buildings that lack warmth and intimacy as an important contributing factor to student alienation. Virtually all suggested solutions or prevention programs include providing metal detectors, video cameras, and security personnel or police—and establishing a caring school environment in which educators know, respect, and connect with kids. Safe schools depend on creating a climate of trust so that our students share with us when either they or a classmate is in distress.

In theory, all educators agree that students need to feel connected. A longitudinal study of 7,000 teenagers found that today's teens are an extremely alienated generation. They spend more time alone than previous generations, few claim to have best friends, and most rank sleep as their most preferred activity (Schneider & Stevenson, 1999).

Though it's easy to point to schools as the leading

cause behind this change in teenagers' attitudes, the reality of school violence and student disaffection is that there are indeed many culprits. As one writer suggests, "The normal culture of adolescence today contains elements that are so nasty that it becomes hard for parents (and professionals) to distinguish between what in a teenager's talk, dress and taste in music, films and video games indicates psychological trouble and what is simply a sign of the times" (Garbarino, 1999, p. 51). Violence among youth is scary and tragic, no matter what the circumstances, no matter how advantaged or disadvantaged the youth.

Although many factors are certainly related to safety and school success, there is no doubt that achievement is most apt to occur in a friendly, predictable classroom atmosphere guided by an enthusiastic teacher who "connects" with students and encourages them to create, take risks, and share ideas. Yet middle and high schools are increasingly performance-based bastions of facts that pressure both educators and students to prove through high-stakes tests that education is really happening.

Despite their increased capacity for abstract reasoning, secondary school students often report fewer opportunities for decision making and lower levels of cognitive involvement than they had in elementary school. At the same time, children must contend with a more complex social environment, including the switch from in-depth contact with a single teacher (in elementary school) to brief contact with many teachers (in secondary school). I recently attended an open house at my daughter's middle school, a place that usually ranks near the top of regional test-score reports. At the open house, each teacher comfortably described her curriculum and expectations, but not one talked about children or asked for questions from their parents. By contrast, my daughter's elementary school had been a warm, involving organization that seemed to value the students themselves more than their performance.

It is troubling for any student to feel disconnected, but shocking that even successful, articulate students who are involved in school activities report feeling a lack of connection between themselves and school adults, frequently describing their relationships as "us versus them" (Dwyer & Skiba, 1999). We can learn from those schools that have successfully short circuited the violent plans of their students. In all such instances, concerned students told trusted and "connected" school adults about their distressed peers, and proper steps were taken before serious problems occurred.

We live in an era that too often places educators in a no-win situation. With teacher accountability increasingly tied to student success as gauged by test performance, many educators experience great stress in simultaneously getting kids to perform while addressing the burdens caused by a toxic world that so often impedes student learning. Politicians and ivory-tower professionals are forever seeking the quick fix, supported by well-intentioned yet often preoccupied and guilt-prone parents, themselves eager to avoid responsibility for their children's failures. Many educators are astounded by the parental enabling behavior that excuses students from responsibility, or by the lack of support from the parents for either the teacher or their child. The result of these cultural realities is that educators are held accountable for student success without regard for the many personal and social conditions that affect it.

Public schools are the only community institution that must receive and educate every child within their boundaries: every learning, physically, and emotionally disabled child; everyone who is abused, neglected, undernourished, or without guidance; every substance-abusing child; and any child who was affected in utero by a drug-using mother. At the same time that we are awed by the great technological achievements that occur daily—and seem to offer great advances in medicine, education, and communication—children are more alienated than ever. We are witnessing a sense of alienation and apathy expressed through high-risk sexual activity, drug and alcohol abuse, violence, depression, gang affiliation, and various forms of self-mutilation, including excessive body piercing. The challenge for educators to *achieve high standards* in a *differentiated classroom*

while addressing *multiple intelligences* in an *inclusive* environment is enormous. Is it any wonder that many veteran teachers are counting the days until retirement, while many new ones doubt that they will teach for more than a few years?

All these factors and demands lead many educators to believe that they simply do not have the time it takes to "connect" with kids, because of the time taken from academics. Yet we know that the need to belong is as essential to learning as the need for food is to survival. A wise philosophical maxim suggests that students will only care what we think when they think that we care. The student who feels isolated or lonely invests more of his energy in seeking friends than in learning theorems. Maslow (1971) believed that most emotional illness and social maladjustment were related to the failure to gratify the basic human need to belong. Virtually every subsequent researcher and most practitioners who work with at-risk youth have shared similar findings, and some have offered a framework through which educators can address this basic need (Brendtro, Brokenleg, & Van Bockern, 1990; Glasser, 1990; Mendler, 1992; Mendler & Curwin, 1999). For us to truly succeed with our students, we must create schools and classrooms that are rich with warmth and nourishment for the mind and for the spirit.

Why This Book? ~

The book provides practical and school-friendly "connection" strategies that teachers can easily integrate into the daily rituals, procedures, and demands of the classroom. The bigger picture is that we need smaller, warmer, theme-oriented secondary schools of no more than 900 students with integrated, multi-disciplinary curricula to help students connect their learning so that they view school as a relevant place. Creating this reality is beyond the scope of any one educator, since it requires visionary leadership, community support, and lots of money. It is also beyond the scope of this book.

Today educators are pressed for time and saddled with many loads. This book offers specific, concrete strategies and suggested interactions to convey a sense of purpose and worth to students. It offers a guide to help each educator create a personalized refuge of safety and risk-taking for all students: everyone from the unattractive, uncoordinated, nonconforming, introverted nerd who has no interest in attending the pep rally, to the high-achieving scholar, athlete, cheerleader, or actor.

How to Use This Book ~

The book is organized so that we first explore the attitudes, beliefs, and understandings that can effectively guide us to practical strategies to help us connect with most students. Because we are not all alike, it is best to choose those strategies that fit you most comfortably. It is neither necessary nor desirable for all educators to do the same thing, but schools can become more effective, safer places when faculty members are all on the same page.

Read each strategy and try to picture yourself using it in your classroom before you actually act on it. Over time, you will develop your favorites and will likely create some new strategies. Be aware of the kinds of things other people do that make you feel welcome. How do your friends greet you? What characteristics of stores or restaurants that you shop or dine in keep you coming back? When you make mistakes, what kinds of things do others say or do that are helpful? How do they express themselves and convey their support? Which people at your school make you feel comfortable or competent? How do they behave? What are some patterns of behavior that you can use when relating to your students? How can you encourage your students to "relate" more effectively with each other? Use your own experiences to guide you in deciding on or developing strategies that will enable you to connect effectively with your students.

The Cincinnati Federation of Teachers conducted a survey of students at a comprehensive high school and found that only 30 percent of the kids agreed with the statement, "My teacher would miss me if I stopped coming to school." Even more disconcerting, only 21 percent agreed with the statement, "Students at my school care about learning" (Rose, 2000, p. 11). It is up to each of us to make our classrooms and schools oases of caring and relevance in a desert of depersonalization. This book will help show you how.

Identifying Disconnected Students ~

We can't predict with certainty which students are sufficiently disconnected that they could hurt either themselves or others. However, those students exhibit specific identifying kinds of behavior that should warn educators to take notice:

- Social withdrawal
- Recurrent or graphic themes of violence in drawings and writings
- Intolerance and prejudice in either actions or writings
- Chronically being picked on
- Bullying others
- Gang involvement
- Drug and alcohol use
- Threats of violence

Though these signs are generally recognized as indicating a more immediate need for intervention, the fact is that some students who commit acts of violence do not appear to be any more or less inclined than anybody else. In fact, a 2000 U.S. Secret Service report suggested that school officials won't improve their ability to predict shooting rampages on school grounds by examining students' traits or behaviors. The report suggests instead that *school leaders are better served by keeping an ear to the ground for the intentions and threats that student shooters often communicate to their peers.* Because a normal part of being human is to occasionally feel different, uncomfortable, and disconnected, and although most people find nonviolent ways of dealing with their hurt, it is best to assume that each person is capable of behaving violently toward others. School safety seems more assured when those of us who work with kids treat each one in a dignified, respectful way.

Necessary Attitudes and Feelings ~

Overcome Lack of Appeal

People tend to seek out others who share similar values and who look and act in familiar ways. While I can understand that heavy body tattooing or body piercing is a fashion statement, a means to get noticed, or a statement of independence, when I see a student with three piercings of the tongue, a nose ring, eyebrow rings, and punctures throughout her ears, I have a hard time connecting with her. I want to say, "Are you nuts?" or "How could you do that to yourself?" or even "Don't you realize that no sensible employer in his right mind is going to hire you to represent his company?" I'm thinking that this person needs to go to an extreme to get anyone to pay attention. On the emotional level, this is a person I

 find unattractive. Giving in to these personal perceptions and judgments, however, often results in disengagement and even rejection of our students.

Connecting with students means that we must sometimes separate our personal beliefs, judgments, and moral standards from our responsibility to feel compassion and concern for those we find different or perhaps even personally unacceptable. Each of us is an adult who is free to choose friends and avoid people whom we find unappealing. Yet each of us is also an educator; within that role, we do not have the luxury of deciding which kids are worthwhile and which ones are not. We must suspend our conventional thinking while on "company time" if we are to be a positive influence on students who say or do things that make us feel disappointed, angry, or frightened.

See Your Challenging Students as Having Something to Teach You

Mr. Smith was an exceptional high school teacher who was almost universally loved by all his students. Paul was a student who finds a way to turn off virtually every adult he meets. As hard as Mr. Smith tried to connect with him, Paul pushed him away by saying and doing offensive things. Nearing exasperation, Mr. Smith approached him and said,

> Paul, I know that God put you in my class to make me a better teacher and a more patient person. He is reminding me that I still have a way to go in order to be successful in teaching all my students. Hard as I have tried to figure what to say or do that would make you believe that you are a capable student who can achieve great things, it seems that I have so far not succeeded in getting through to you. Are there times that you have done all you know and you don't get the results you want? Have there been people in your life that seem impossible to please no matter how hard you try? What is that like for you? And what do you do when you are faced with this?

Mr. Smith was able to put aside his personal feelings and, as a teacher, realize that maybe Paul had something to teach him. Most "challenging" students provide us with opportunities to learn and practice lessons of *patience, compassion,* and *tolerance.* It is hard for students to stay disconnected when caring, persistent adults reach out to them in ways that convey an eagerness to learn.

Can you think of some students to whom you respond abruptly or angrily? What can you learn about patience, compassion, or tolerance from these students that might make you a better teacher or an even better person than you already are?

Get Past Zero Tolerance

Zero-tolerance policies have become popular as a way of trying to make schools safer. Certainly nothing is more important than a safe school. Of course we need strong, effective policies to protect our students and to help them feel safe; but we must be careful to balance the need for safety with the ability to evaluate each situation based on its own special circumstances. We need to replace simple formulas with the kinds of knowledge and intuition that keep our schools safe—yet allow troubled students to make mistakes and learn from them.

When enforced to the letter, zero tolerance can lead to unnecessary suspensions or expulsions that may do little more than further alienate already disenfranchised youth. Suspensions for carrying a plastic knife in a backpack or forgetfully carrying a nail file are rarely necessary. Even more complicated cases require the use of analysis and judgment. A 6th grader was expelled from school for having made up a "hit list" of 12 people to kill. His fantasy was quite vivid, although he had neither weapons nor any kind of plan about how he was going to do it. It turned out that the boy was being harassed and beaten at home, was picked on by other kids at school, and had had dog manure thrown at him. Certainly, his behavior constituted a real threat, and school authorities had every right to be vigilant in attending to this issue. Unfortunately, by limiting their actions to expulsion and a report to the police, school administrators and teachers never actually engaged this boy in any way. Had they done so, they could easily have learned of his deep pain and begun to deal with it, as well as those responsible for causing his misery.

Rather than simply following formulas, teachers and administrators can use their knowledge and intuition to penetrate to the deeper issues affecting student behavior. As noted in a prior book (Curwin & Mendler, 1997), we must be "as tough as necessary" rather than "zero tolerant." Expelling students without first engaging them in any sort of communication can lead to a deepening of hatred and may make angry students even more dangerous.

Stay Optimistic and Be Persistent

People revisit their old ways many times as they acquire new behaviors. Students who present themselves as defiant, obnoxious, or distant are unlikely to let go of these behaviors easily. Keep in mind that people continue the behaviors that work for them to get what they think they need. An emotionally distant student who believes that anonymity will keep him safe from high expectations is unlikely to respond quickly to a teacher's effort to connect. It takes greater persistence, guided by optimism, to break through these barriers of perceived safety to develop bonds of trust.

We educators must have an unflagging belief in

the capacity of people to change. Health research has found that an optimistic view helps people cope with disease better and live longer. There is little doubt that sustained optimism is also a powerful tool that can influence others. Our belief that our efforts can and will make a difference should, however, be tempered by the realization that the process of change is often slow and unsteady.

Build on Strengths Instead of Trying to Fix Deficits

It can be much easier to build connections with students when we see the glass of opportunity as half full rather than half empty. Changing the way we think about certain students and their behaviors opens the door to far more positive interactions with them—even bonding. For example, if we label a student who gives us a hard time as "stubborn" or "disobedient," then our reaction will invariably be negative, and we are likely to regularly butt heads with this student. However, if we view that same student as "determined" or "persistent," we are more apt to convey respect; most adults admire children who project these qualities. In fact, students who direct these qualities toward their schoolwork are usually highly successful. Moving our characterization from "stubborn" to "persistent" enables us to avoid a likely power struggle or a battle of wills while allowing us to acknowledge the student's assertiveness as a strength that might even be redirected. If we view a "defiant" student as "courageous" or "strong willed," we might build a bond rather than become the enemy.

We can even change the way we respond to misbehavior. When a "strong-willed" student refuses to do as asked, you can say,

> I have a lot of respect for how you stand up for yourself. There are many times in life when it's necessary to say no and refuse to do what someone says. If someone important told you to jump off a roof, I have no doubt that you would be able to think for yourself and refuse. With your kind of determination, I have no doubt that you can achieve whatever you want, including handling this class. It isn't easy, but then again you've succeeded in handling lots of things that aren't easy, haven't you?

Virtually every negative behavior has a positive corre-
late. The "class clown" can be viewed as a humorist
who helps to keep things light. A tardy student can be
viewed as being present. The "worst of the worst" can
be seen as the "toughest of the tough" who has had to
defend himself against a hostile world that has tried
to take advantage of him. When we reframe negative
behavior and attitudes, it opens the door to the sharing of appreciation, rather than the exacerbation of
conflict.

Value Your Relationship with Your Students as an Important Tool in Helping Them Achieve "Standards"

Many educators wonder how they are going to
find the time to build and sustain relationships with
students when there are so many demands for
achievement. It is a mistake to see it as an either/or
proposition. In fact, successful educators realize that a
strong relationship with students leads to better discipline in the classroom, which means more time for
instruction. In addition, students who are unmoti-
vated toward the subject you teach are more apt to be
motivated if they respect you and know you care

about them. For non-intrinsically motivated students to meet academic standards, they need adequate challenges with meaningful feedback from a thoughtful adult who is honest and caring.

Make the Classroom Safe from Physical Danger and Embarrassment

Fear of harm or embarrassment creates a threat, which shuts down learning and increases defensiveness, anxiety, and posturing. Students must therefore feel safe not only for their physical well-being, but also for being able to make mistakes without embarrassment. A richly encouraging environment that emphasizes basics while promoting innovation leads to engaged, motivated learners.

Three Types of Connections

Having a long-term, close relationship with a caring, responsible parent or other adult dramatically increases the likelihood of success in life for at-risk youth (Rutter, 1990; Seita, Mitchell, & Tobin, 1996; Werner & Smith, 1992). Success for all students is based on intellectual or academic and social competence. Hence, this book provides strategies that show

how the responsible educator can develop a *personal* connection so that *academic* and *social* competence can flourish, as follows:

- Personal connection means finding ways to create an atmosphere of trust, so that students want to learn what we have to share.

- Academic connection strategies offer many ways to encourage success in content areas. Students will not connect with school unless they believe that they can succeed.

- Social connections among students convert the barriers that often divide us into bridges that link students with each other—and with the adults in their lives.

Strategies for Developing Personal Connection ~

Collect personal index cards. It is wise to get to know your students as soon as possible. Several teachers have found it effective to give each student a 3" x 5" index card, and have them list such things as their favorite sport, after-school activity, food, school subject, or previous favorite teacher. There are endless questions that can be asked that will quickly enable you to get to know your students. Create a list of questions pertaining to issues, experiences, or preferences that you think your students would find interesting.

Smile! A friendly smile can go a long way toward making someone believe that she is special. It takes little effort but has a big payoff. Conventional thinking suggests that a smile is just an expression of happiness; but research has found that people who smile can actually make themselves feel happier. Some researchers have even found that people can make themselves healthier by smiling and laughing (Cousins, 1980).

The message is: Don't wait to feel good before you smile—smile and good feelings will follow.

Say "good morning" to every student you see in the hall. This is another simple gesture that takes no more time than walking through the halls in an anonymous, impersonal way, but can yield huge results in defining yourself as approachable. Make eye contact and, with a friendly smile on your face, offer a warm greeting. If you are so inclined, you might want to confront students who ignore you by responding in a friendly manner. I have walked down many high school halls and said hello to students and received no acknowledgment from them. I have trained myself to not take it personally when students don't respond. Instead, I have become comfortable turning around, following them and then saying something like

> I said hello to you and you didn't answer me. I just wanted to let you know that it feels really good when busy people like you take the time to notice and answer back with a hello.

Be at the door and greet students as they arrive. It is best to personalize your greeting by including the

WELCOME! student's name. Students appreciate knowing that their teacher knows who they are.

Send home birthday cards. Nowadays it is simple to record birth dates on a computer database so that it is relatively easy to keep track of birthdays and acknowledge them with cards. It is best to hand write the student's name and personally sign the card. Most schools will even pay the postage.

Keep pictures of your family or friends posted in class. This acknowledges you as having a life outside of school and shows that you value important people in your life. Some students will enjoy knowing that they can experience a sense of family in your presence. It can also work well to share with students those characteristics of your children that remind you of certain students. This can be particularly beneficial when you conclude by seeking advice. For example,

I sometimes have difficulty getting my son—who is about your age—to do his homework. What seems to work well with you that I might be able to do?

Ask an opinion from a student who rarely offers anything. This is an empowering behavior that is greatly appreciated, although not always acknowledged, by the student. There are many ways to do this. One of my favorites is to approach the student as she is leaving class and say, "I don't hear from you too often in class, but you look very focused and thoughtful. I was wondering what you thought about _____ . Thanks for sharing."

An even better approach is to share the student's opinion with the whole class. Unless the student has given you permission to do so, it is generally best to do this anonymously ("I got this great idea from one of you that I think is going to make our class work even better than it already does. . . . ").

Do the "2 x 10." Think of a student you find unattractive. Make a commitment to invest two uninterrupted, undivided minutes a day for 10 consecutive days to "relationship build." If it is impossible to follow this guideline, then try to get as close to meeting it as possible. During these two minutes, you cannot do or say anything related to correcting the student's behavior or telling the student what he must do differently to be successful in class. Anything else that is within proper moral and ethical guidelines is allowed. Expect awkwardness and abrupt communication during the first few days: Most students will be wary of your intentions, and you are unlikely to feel comfortable about knowing what to say or do. By the 10th day, most teachers report improved communication with the student, as well as evidence of better behavior.

Use the 4H method. Naddie Jones, a high school teacher in Athens, Georgia, thinks about which of her students she knows the least. After compiling a list, she greets these students daily with one of four welcoming "H's": handshake, high five, "how are you?" (asks), "hello" (says). Jones reports that many "tough" kids eventually open up and connect after she does this for a while. A related method is known as the "H or H" ("hug" or "handshake"; Mendler, 1997; Mendler & Curwin, 1999). Essentially, the H or H in its pure form is primarily designed for use with younger children. In this method, the teacher greets children at the door with either a hug or handshake. Each student decides her preference.

Recently, a teacher of 9th graders shared that she did the hug or handshake at the end of every class. She went on to say,

> Yesterday we were going to the library. Before we left the room to go there, a student asked, "Do we have to do the hug or handshake?" He is 15 years old and was very much aware that 70 other students besides his class were going to be in the library. Almost the entire class bombarded him with, "Hey! We want our handshake." He shook mine when he left.

Think aloud. Share ideas and conflicts aloud with the class, especially when choices aren't absolutely clear. You can do this with academic or interpersonal conflict. For example, when you hear inappropriate language, you might say,

> Whoa, when I hear words that sound disrespectful, there is a part of me that wants to argue and yell, and another equally strong part that wants to try to understand why it is that we sometimes forget where we are and what is appropriate. Hard as it is, I am going to continue behaving like an adult and get on with the lesson.

On the academic side, you could say, "I sense that some are bored with this unit, and actually so am I. But we need to get through it, so I appreciate your hanging in there."

Offer notes of appreciation. It is remarkable how much goodwill and cooperation can be gained from students by writing notes to them about something you appreciate. A simple thank-you note in the form of an index card or sticky note is all that is needed. Perhaps the easiest thing to do is to simply thank the student in writing for cooperative behavior. Try a thank-you note to a student who often is tardy but comes to class on time one day. In fact, you might want to make a list of all the "regular," appropriate little things that students do that are rarely noticed or generally taken for granted (getting their homework done; following class rules; behaving in a courteous way), and periodically write a thank-you note to the student about those behaviors. Keep your list handy as a reminder.

Give occasional "positive paradoxical" notes.
With some of your more difficult students, you can
often influence their behavior by giving them a positive note shortly after they have done something
inappropriate. Like a fastball pitcher who surprises an
expectant batter with a slow change-up, doing the
opposite of what a student expects can lead to a positive result.

For example, Joey L. is horsing around with his
buddies in the back of the class. Mr. Smith approaches
him with a stern look and a prewritten note (not in
an envelope or in an unsealed envelope), and tells
him to give the note to his mother. Mr. Smith walks
away. Naturally, Joey peeks at the note, expecting crit-
ical comments. The note reads:

Dear Ms. _____ ,
I have had the pleasure of having your son Joey in
my class these last few weeks, and I find him to
be an enthusiastic boy who is full of life. Joey is
one of the more popular students and loves to
socialize, and while I occasionally need to remind
him to settle down, he adds a spark to our class
that I really appreciate.

Sincerely,
Mr. Smith

Allow students to "borrow" personal artifacts.
Relationships deepen when people share special experiences or things. If a student is involved in an ath-
letic competition, you might lend her your "lucky"
swatch of cloth. If you know of a student's musical
taste through his comments or T-shirt, you can lend a
CD that you own as a way of seeking the student's
opinion or to simply share a common interest.

**Develop "cueing" signals with troubled stu-
dents.** Many problems escalate when the teacher and
student want to "save face." When conflicts occur,
both the educator and the student need to feel in
charge and respected by all onlookers. Respect can be
gained by agreeing in advance to special warning signals or gestures that each can use with the other
when patience is growing thin. Before the next conflict, meet with the student and explain that you
know that both you and he are looking for respect
and neither of you wants to "look bad" in front of
everyone else. Brainstorm some relatively subtle gestures or signals that you can give to alert the other
person in a respectful way to step back and avoid a
conflict. For example, a "C" hand gesture can stand
for "chill," "calm down," "cooperate," or "can do."
You can develop acronyms that represent expected
behaviors or a cessation of undesirable behavior: for

example, "ZYL" (zip your lip), "KIO" (knock it off), or "GMF" (give me five).

Play their music occasionally. With some particularly difficult classes, you can use music as an incentive for behaving or completing an assignment. Middle school educator B. Mayberry tape records songs that are popular with students. Whenever students talk without permission, she plays the tape until the talking stops. At the end of the week, if music is still left, students can talk with their friends for however long there is music left playing on the tape. If there is no music left, there is no sanctioned socializing. As an alternative, you can simply play students' expressed musical preferences from time to time as a show of respect and connection.

Acknowledge a personal imperfection (behavior or personality). Teenagers are characteristically preoccupied with how other people see them. Although aging has its pitfalls, one of its benefits is that we often are far less concerned with impressing others than we were as kids. It can be refreshing and reassuring for your students to see a respected adult make mistakes, acknowledge them, and even rejoice in them from time to time.

Be a chaperone. Supervising an after-school activity or trip can provide many opportunities to connect with students in ways that are often unavailable in the classroom. It can be a great way to interact with those kids who may lack interest or competence in a particular class but who shine in other areas of interest.

Thank them for cooperating even before they have. A powerful tool for both connecting with students and influencing their behavior is to thank them for their effort or cooperation even before you see it. For example, Bob is interrupting class. Mr. Hanks says to him, "Bob, thanks for waiting your turn and giving others a chance to share beginning right now. I really appreciate it." Most students find compliance irresistible if you've already thanked them.

Notice writings/drawings with unusual or unique themes. Many times students convey thoughts and feelings through writings, drawings, and images. Comments on these, offering an impression or asking a question, can build a relationship. I remember Dmitra, an angry young woman whose idea of communication with teachers was either a flick of her middle finger or a four-letter word. Ms. Johnson, her English teacher, noticed that Dmitra was doodling what appeared to be boats:

Ms. Johnson: Those look like boats, Dmitra. Is that what they are?

Dmitra: No, they ain't no boats!

Ms. Johnson: Well, when I look at your drawing, I get a feeling of movement, like going places. Do you ever think about going to other places?

Dmitra: All the time. Especially when I'm in this _____ ing class.

Ms. Johnson: I know it must take a lot of effort for you to come here especially when you would much rather be other places. Where are some other places you would like to visit if you could?

Dmitra: [long pause] The street corner for some stuff or the smoke shop for some smokes.

Ms. Johnson: Hmm. I get the picture. You like to do things your own way in your own time. Do you ever think about getting away from here and visiting some other place where you could feel as free as you'd like?

Dmitra: All the time.

Ms. Johnson: Where would you go if you could?

Dmitra: Probably Hawaii.

Ms. Johnson: Ever been there?

Dmitra: Nah, but it sure would be nice.

Ms. Johnson followed by asking Dmitra questions about whether she'd like to go to Hawaii alone or with others. If she were there, what would she do that she couldn't do here? Ms. Johnson was able to broaden her relationship with Dmitra by focusing on doodles that could easily have been ignored. It is just as appropriate, although certainly more unsettling, to engage someone about disturbing or violent images through exploratory questioning. Not only can it establish a relationship, it can also aid in identifying seriously troubled young people who may be in con- siderable distress and who could harm themselves or others.

Sponsor a personal initiative. Connections with students can deepen while a teacher is sponsoring, organizing, or simply participating in a commu- nity-oriented initiative. Brainstorm with the class about various charities or causes that need support, create a plan together, and then implement it. Some possibilities include selling a product to raise funds, performing a service, or organizing a campaign or event, such as a walk-a-thon. If you prefer participa- tion to organization, let your students know the cause you support and invite them to get involved. The extension of holiday season giving (through the recognition of diverse holidays like Kwanzaa, Christ-mas, Hanukkah, and Ramadan), which many schools embrace, can provide students with ongoing opportu-nities to feel good about themselves while giving to others. During the holiday season, many schools seem to automatically encourage students to help those who are less fortunate. The chorus entertains at a senior citizens' home; the student council initiates clothing or food drives for the needy; and the par-ent-teacher organization gets everyone to join neigh-borhood beautification projects, such as cleaning or repairing playgrounds and parks. Encouraging and involving your students in efforts like these *throughout the school year* is a great way to provide community benefit while strengthening your connection with your kids.

Establish predictable rules and routines. Though they may not like the actual rules, students feel safe when adults set limits. Rules should be based on the values and principles educators need for the learning process to take place. Involving students in the rule-making process can make them feel more con-nected to you. All rules, routines, and procedures that are compatible with the school's principles or values can be accepted. For example, because educators know that there can be no effective learning unless the environment is safe, we must promote values such as "School must be a safe place," "All staff and students are expected to take care of the place," and "Show respect for yourself and others." Students are then invited to propose rules or procedures that are compatible with these values.

Each week, ask students to share one thing that you can do better for them and tell individuals or the class one thing they can do better for you. In writing, during private conversation, or both, ask a student with whom you are having difficulties to share with you one suggestion for how you could help him feel better about coming to class or how to be successful in school. At first, make this a one-way street—ask the student for suggestions, and listen. Unless the request is outrageous or entirely inappropriate, work hard to comply. As Steven Covey (1989) suggests, "Give first before you get." The next step is to tell the student one thing that he could do to make things better for you. This strategy can also be applied to a whole class or a subgroup within the class.

Make up double-initial nicknames (the "Smooth Sam" method). Create a nickname for as many students as you can. Try to make the nickname fit a telling characteristic of the student. One teacher we know develops double-initial nicknames. Examples are Smooth Sam, Tom the Titan, Lucky Lilly, or Jurassic John. Nicknames are fun and make people feel special, as long as they are respectful and affectionate. Keep them fun, but polite, and students will enjoy it and feel included.

Create acronym nicknames. Darryl A., a Chicago-area middle school teacher, writes positive, affirming words next to each letter of a student's name. Then each week, he writes one student's name on a large poster and encourages fellow classmates to write positive characteristics and adjectives associated with that student. Examples are: SAM = Successful, Able, Mature; MARY = Magnificent, Awesome, Real, Your good friend.

Call a student at home and share feedback. One of the most powerful ways to convey importance to a student is to call her at home. Without an audience around, that student is much more likely to really listen to and appreciate your feedback. In particular, educators are likely to have much better results discussing disruptive behaviors with students in this manner. Discussion can begin with something like

Danielle, this is Ms. Jones calling to share some information with you that is difficult to do during class. I thought this would be a good time for me to better understand what you think you need to be more successful in class, and to share what I'd like to see more from you.

To avoid any appearance of impropriety, speak with the student after first informing her parent(s) about the purpose of your call.

Encourage your students to keep a journal. Let your students know that you understand that every day they are likely to have thoughts, feelings, and experiences that affect how they think and what they do. There may not always be either time or desire to share this information directly with others, but it can be helpful to keep track of the kinds of things that influence behavior and decision-making. Encourage students to keep a journal of important experiences, thoughts, or feelings. Let them know that they can keep these just for themselves or share them with you. If there are any specifics that they would prefer you not read, they can fold or staple those pages.

Call parents (or send home a note) complimenting their child. A simple phone call to a parent or a brief note complimenting some aspect of the student's performance or achievement can help gain support from the parent and build rapport with the student. This doesn't take much time in these days of voicemail and e-mail. An introductory letter home to parents describing yourself, your class, and how parents can get in touch with you if the need arises can also engender parental support.

Visit the cafeteria and eat lunch with a student who appears disconnected. If once a week is too much, then do this periodically. Sharing a meal together is one of the best ways to connect with anyone. If nothing else, you can talk about how good or bad the food is.

Greet using a rating scale (1–5). As students arrive, you might offer your impressions of how they are carrying themselves. For example,

> Maria, you seem kind of bummed out today. On a scale of 1 to 5, with one being a lousy day and a five being a great one, where are you?

Share a high-five or an "all right!" with students in the "3 to 5" range. Offer support by asking if there is anything that you can quickly do to help move the day up a slot or two, or simply offer a comment like "I hope things get better from here." You can create a chart that provides another way of encouraging your students to either express themselves or seek support if they want (see Figure 1). The chart can be presented daily or weekly, depending on how often you see your students.

Apologize when you *blow it and know it,* and even when you don't know it. A sincere apology is a powerful way to communicate that you care. It is easier to do when you "blow it and know it." Unfortunately, we often see students whose anger or apathy may have a different source. They might feel sad or disappointed about something that happened at home or on the way to school, but they may take it out on us by acting disrespectful or angry. Although we are not the source of their agitation, unless we address it, their negativism is likely to remain or even worsen. When you experience negativity from a student, it can help to say something like this:

> Daquan, I must have done something to bother you, so let me apologize for whatever that may have been. I hope you will help me understand

~ FIGURE 1 ~

The "Kind of Day I Am Having" Chart

Name (Optional) _____

1. Put a circle around the number that best shows the kind of day (week) you are having.

10   9   8   7   6   5   4   3   2   1

Great   **Okay**   **Lousy**

2. The things that are happening today (this week) to make me feel the way I do are

_____ .

_____ .

_____ .

3. Would you like to talk things over with either me or a counselor? _____ yes   _____ no what I said or did so that I can be more tuned in next time.

Usually, students will next respond by saying, "Nah, it's not you—there's just a lot of stuff going on."

You can conclude, "Let me know if I can be helpful with any of that stuff."

Notice when someone is acting differently and acknowledge it. There are many ways to convey this. For example, say, "You aren't being your cheery self today. Is anything wrong?" or "It must be a tough day today, you're not acting like your usual self." This strategy can also be used when the student isn't really acting all that differently, but you want to acknowledge a more positive aspect of the student's behavior or personality. For example, even if Joe is obnoxious 75 percent of the time, you might want to help him improve the quality of the 25 percent of his time that he is relatively pleasant. So you might say, "Joe, your lack of interest is telling me that you are just not being yourself today. I hope your day gets better beginning right now."

Show up at an event that involves them (and bring a special token of recognition). Your presence at a student event goes a long way toward showing that you care. Sometimes it might be appropriate to bring a token of appreciation, such as flowers or an inexpensive gift relating to the event. Another nice touch is to send a congratulatory card or note that recognizes the student's involvement and achievement.

Notice absence (phone, e-mail, fax, or note). Kids who feel that nobody cares often believe that they are unnoticed. When students are absent, send a note or fax, or call them at home to tell them you noticed they weren't in school. It also gives you an opportunity to tell them what they missed and perhaps engage with the student who might be having problems learning in your class. For example, you might share a tip that would help the student get back to class. In essence, the message is, "You weren't in class and you were missed!"

Be protective. Unfortunately, some schools seem to exist for the well-being of people other than students. Although most schoolpeople talk as if they are in business for students, practices that conflict with that philosophy do occur. Examples include administrators or teachers who value procedures or rules more than those they are designed to benefit—the students; adults who criticize students and each other publicly in a disrespectful way; or colleagues who won't put differences of philosophy aside to do what is best for students. Sadly, the energy of caring educators in these schools is slowly drained until many burn out.

A key symptom of a "toxic" school is when many adults feel disconnected, with a pervasive sense of dread replacing their former enthusiasm. These schools often have sensitive educators who feel unsupported and unappreciated. Educators who work in such schools must surround themselves with at least some colleagues who stay focused on what is best for students. This gives teachers a better chance of staying emotionally alive and professionally vital. Working in a toxic school is certainly bad for an educator who wants a fulfilling career, but attending such a school can be even worse for students whose educational lives are on the line.

Have fun together. Laughter is a wonderful thing! Remember that those who laugh the most live the longest. Allow yourself to have fun with your students. Teach at least one thing you love every day to each of your classes. Your enthusiasm will become contagious, and your students will look forward to coming to your class.

Offer personal "best" awards. On an informal basis, congratulate students' even small triumphs by giving them a "certificate of success." The possibilities are endless. Certificates can be given for academic or behavioral improvement. Another option is to offer some kind of surprise reward. For example, a candy bar can be given to a student, along with a note that thanks him for making a special effort. (If you'd prefer not to give candy, give something else that the student might like that is inexpensive but shows that you gave some thought to what he might like.)

Figure 2 presents important questions to reflect on as you develop personal connections with students.

Strategies for Developing Academic Connection ~

Take photos of students as they are working on projects. Photograph students engaged in various classroom activities that range from sitting in a seat to working on a project. These pictures can be displayed as classroom "art."

Congratulate five students each class on something they achieved. Sometime between the beginning of class and the end, notice at least a small

~ FIGURE 2 ~

Questions for the Educator to Help Develop Personal Connection

1. Do I believe that the student I currently see is all he or she will become? (A fixed view will lock you into snap judgments about which students are worth your time and which ones are not.)

2. Do I believe that people change? (Unless you do, you are not going to be able to influence change.)

3. Do I realize that reaching my most challenging student is what being a professional educator is all about? (If not you, then who?)

4. Do I truly believe that the students I teach are more important than the content that I am teaching? (Are you willing to adapt or even suspend the prescribed curriculum when it is clear that students are not learning?)

accomplishment that a student has achieved. A short verbal notice or written note is all it takes. Make an effort to do this with at least five different students during each class.

Ask a nonparticipating student an open-ended question. Many students disengage academically because they believe they can't achieve. Others withdraw because they think their friends may see them as "uncool" if they are smart. Nonparticipating students will often be more willing to risk getting involved when asked open-ended, less factually based questions. For example, an unsure or insecure student is more apt to answer a question that asks for an opinion or calls for imagination rather than one that asks for a fact. Asking what one might do if faced with the same circumstances confronted by George Washington at Valley Forge, for example (freezing temperatures, little food, low morale) is more likely to get students involved than asking who it was that

Washington and his troops were about to fight. Sometimes it's even best to let all students know that there is not a single correct answer to a particular question and that you are looking for them to consider alternatives.

Respond nonevaluatively at least three times per class. When students answer questions with something other than what you consider the "right" answer, make your next response nonjudgmental at least three times each class. Offer comments like "Good try," "That's an interesting way of looking at it," or "That's unique but different from what I was actually looking for."

Offer adequate wait time. After asking a question, wait at least 10 seconds after calling on someone before you either make a comment or ask for another student's point of view. Let students know about the rule, and that they needn't even raise their hands until the appropriate "wait time" has passed.

Consult faculty. If you continue to have trouble connecting with a particularly elusive student who seems to want to remain "anonymous," ask colleagues if they have any information that could help you. Try to find out what strengths or interests the student has that you might address.

Give humorous "recognitions of achievement" awards. Although awards for achievement in the form of an assembly or student of the week are common practice, only those students who believe that they are in the race are likely be motivated by them. Rarely does honoring one student's achievement motivate another unless she sees herself as having characteristics, talents, or abilities similar to those of the recognized student. Tongue-in-cheek awards can motivate students who may not be recognized in more traditional ways. For example, at the end of a quarter or report card period, present awards such as "Most Frequent Question-Asker" or "Most Creative Reason for Not Doing an Assignment" to members of your class. Naturally, conveying an attitude of genuinely caring for the student is necessary for this method to be perceived as well-intentioned and fun rather than sarcastic.

Show students they can overcome obstacles. One of the best ways to build an academic connection is to show students that they already have what it takes to meet a challenge and master it. Improvements in both behavior and academic achievement can be encouraged in this way. For example, say,

Bob, I noticed that when Luis and Ben were trying to tease you, you found a way to stay in control. You refused to give up your power to them.

Andrea, you struggled through number 4, which
is a problem about decimals, and got it right.
What did you do to figure it out? It looks like
numbers 5 and 6 could use a similar effort, and
we both know that you can handle them!

Create a class photo album. Take photos of
students engaged in learning and/or while they are
putting forth effort you want to encourage. The photos can decorate the walls and then be replaced with
new ones. The old ones can be put into an album and
kept in the classroom for parents, visitors, and students to see. At the end of the year, this album can be
placed in a central location or display case or kept
with such mementos as yearbooks.

Make mistakes. As I mentioned previously, let
your students see you as imperfect in the subject you
teach. Allow yourself to make mistakes, acknowledge
them, and take steps to correct them. When corrected
by a student, be appreciative and gracious, even
though your tendency may be to get uptight.

Visit a real or virtual place or site you've studied. The more real and tangible you can make learning, the more interested your students are likely to be. Field trips can provide a more hands-on element, as can "virtual" visits on the Internet.

Be characters you've studied. As you are discussing content in class, find ways for you and your students to become the characters that are being studied. Students could take on the role of Lincoln during the Civil War, while others might portray a Southern plantation owner. Making and wearing costumes of the era can be an embellishment that connects students to learning.

Write a daily encouraging or inspiring message. There is little doubt that the messages we feed ourselves influence our behavior. In the same way food's nutrition affects our bodies, the way we talk to ourselves affects our attitude and behavior. Consider posting an encouraging, inspirational, gently humorous, or thought-provoking message on a regular basis. Here are some possibilities:

Attitude is all, and I am in control of my attitude.
If someone bugs me, I won't take it personally.
I care about people and they care about me.

Effort is everything.

I don't have to be the smartest. I am smart enough.

Failure is good, because it shows me one more way that
    doesn't work.

I can't control the wind, but I can adjust my sails.

Stuff happens, but I don't have to step in it.

Next time someone tries to make you feel bad, picture him
    with a bow in his hair and a pacifier in his mouth.

Some sources of inspirational messages you may want to consider are the "Successories" books (e.g., Karvalas, 1998) and many of the volumes of *Chicken Soup for the Soul* (e.g., Canfield, Hansen, & Kirberger, 1997).

Display student work in the classroom. People like to see themselves through their creations. The sad thing is that as students move from elementary to middle and high school, the plainer and more sterile the halls become. Educators at all levels should try to post, display, and exhibit student work on a regular basis—in the classroom, in the halls, in display cases, on easels, in banners, wherever they can.

Specify daily learning objectives. Academic achievement on a daily basis becomes much more likely when students know the specific learning

objectives of each class period. The day's learning
objectives can be posted someplace visible to the
whole class, such as the chalkboard. Identify a few
specific "take aways" that you particularly want your
students to comprehend. Then let them know what
these are.

Begin with the end in mind! For example, say, "By
the end of today's class, you will know why it is best
to reduce fractions to their lowest common denomi-
nator." Before the end of class, refer back to the objective and ask students to demonstrate their knowledge
in some format. You can vary the format, using
"think-pair-share" one day, small-group sharing
another, two written sentences conveying under-
standing yet another day, and so on.

Finally, let students know where, how, and from
whom they can get help if there are gaps in their mas-
tery of the objective.

**Connect the content with current issues of
meaning.** People are likely to learn more when they
can relate to or have feelings about what is being
taught. At least once a week (more often if possible),
challenge yourself to use issues that directly relate to
the lives and interests of your students while teaching
your subject. For example, if you are a math teacher,

use word problems that use contemporary music groups, or create a problem-solving situation that you are confident your students face.

Plan a lesson from the perspective of your least capable students. As you are planning a lesson, consider those students who you think have a good chance of failing to master the material you plan to teach. Who are they? Why do you think they will have trouble? Is the material too abstract? Is someone too distracted to sit and listen long enough to get it? Might there be too much writing required for some students? Are some unable to independently follow all the steps necessary for success? Do some students need more in-depth explanations before they can proceed?

Use adapting techniques to broaden success. Most classes contain students with a broad range of background and skills. It is not unusual to have gifted students as well as students with learning disabilities in the same academic setting. With such differences in the abilities of students to work and perform, educators must adapt the techniques used in the classroom. Many of these adaptations can easily be implemented without dramatically changing the way instruction occurs and performance is measured.

For example, you can adapt the *number of items* that a student is expected to learn. All students can be required to complete whichever 5 problems (out of 10) best show they understand the material. You can offer bonus credits or points that students can "bank" if they do more than the basic set of requirements. You can also adapt the *time* allotted for the assignment, with extra time allowed for classwork, extended time limits for tests, or untimed tests. You can adapt *participation* by having one student share while another listens. You can adapt the *degree of support* provided to students; for example, students can be assigned to "check" groups, in which the group is responsible for ensuring that each member has successfully completed a task. Students can be paired with "tutorial buddies." Some students benefit from a daily outline of the most important concepts to be learned. Others feel more academically connected when they can express their knowledge in less conventional ways, such as drawing, dramatizing, singing, or rapping. Students with writing difficulties can be allowed to explain an answer to you before putting it on paper.

Learn from them. Put your students in charge of teaching the class occasionally. You might assign components of a unit to different groups. More often, you could ask students to analyze and synthesize the information you teach by pairing them up and encouraging them to teach and review with each other. This peer teaching can be particularly effective for test preparation. True learning is demonstrated only when somebody can share knowledge with others.

Use e-mail to communicate with students and parents. Let your students and their parents know that you will use e-mail or the school Web site to post daily assignments, as well as long-term projects and their due dates.

Limit pop quizzes. Pop quizzes contribute unnecessarily to anxiety and rarely lead to increased competence. In fact, the sudden wave of fear that an unexpected test elicits can quickly shut down learning and memory, leading to poorer performance. Tell your students that you won't play games with them. You will let them know of all upcoming tests well in advance so that they can allocate sufficient time for study and seek help if needed.

Require an "I learned" log. On a daily, weekly, or even biweekly basis, ask students to share either academic or personal insights that they have had. It is helpful to provide them with a brief summary of key concepts you are studying—particularly those requiring analysis or synthesis. For example, if your class is studying the Civil War, you might ask them to summarize how the Battle of Gettysburg turned the tide toward the Union. Suggest that they explore how a "battle" they are currently having with someone important or within themselves can turn out successfully. Does one side *always* have to lose for the other side to win? At the end of the Civil War, do you think it was right for the Union to help rebuild the South, rather than punish it? Is there a lesson about "humility" and "healing" that we can learn here? Students can keep track of important learning moments related to academic content that are connected to personal and academic growth. As an incentive, you can offer bonus credit for submissions that meet criteria identified in advance.

Answer up to three questions each period that are irrelevant to the content, and invite students to see you when it is convenient for you to answer any others. Some students dominate class with questions that are either off task or, at best, loosely related to the content. Such questions are distracting and annoying, and interfere with the continuity of learning. Instead of answering all off-task questions or shutting students down by refusing to answer any, identify a limited number that you will try to answer during class. If there are more, explain that students will need to set up an appointment with you to answer them. You could say,

> We have lots to cover today, and I am sure that some of you may have questions. If your question is a good one, but it is not the right time for me to answer, I will let you know. See me after class, and I will then either give you an answer or tell you when I plan to answer the question.

Give a rain-check. This variation of postponing the answer to a question lets students know that you will issue rain-checks for any questions that you will answer, just at a different time. When you give students rain-checks, ask them to write down the question. Collect all written questions at the end of class, and either answer them then or let students know when you plan to provide an answer.

Be curious together. Learning involves grappling with the challenges of not knowing. Express curiosity when issues come up that defy simplistic solutions.

Even when students ask a question you've heard a hundred times before, express enthusiasm while exploring and answering. The following "openers" can be helpful ways of supporting student motivation:

"How interesting. I hadn't thought of it exactly that way before."

"I hear your excitement in solving that problem. It feels good when it all comes together, doesn't it?"

"You are really curious about _____ , and that gets my juices flowing. Thanks."

"Some of you look curious and confused. Don't worry. Eventually it will make sense."

Have an "on-a-roll" program. You can encourage your students to compete against themselves by developing an "on-a-roll" program. Patterned after the usual "honor roll," in which only the highest academic achievers are recognized, the "on-a-roll" program acknowledges all students for demonstrating improved effort, performance, or achievement. Recognition can be either public (such as a weekly reading of qualifying student names, placement in a classroom newsletter, or adding names on a classroom chart) or private (such as a congratulatory "You've been on a roll" note sent home to the student and the parent).

Refuse to be biased by standardized test scores. Research by Rosenthal and Jacobson (1968) found that teacher expectations were more important than student ability or aptitude in determining academic excellence. In that study, teachers were told that a pretest had identified a special group of students who were "spurters" or "bloomers," from whom greater intellectual growth was expected. In fact, the identified students were randomly selected, and their academic performance was matched against a control group. Significant intellectual growth was measured among those designated as "special." Too many bright students are denied access to stimulating academic programs because of insufficient performance on standardized tests. Teachers must stress to all students that the key ingredients for determining success are effort and a strong work ethic.

Figure 3 suggests questions for reflection on developing academic connections.

Consider offering bonus points for homework. Even though students' grades suffer when they don't do homework, many teachers still have trouble convincing their students to do it. In many classes, homework is a requirement that "counts" for a certain percentage of a grade. In my view, homework is simply a means toward an end. A good homework assignment is suggested for the following purposes:

- *Practice* (learning the information)
- *Application* (using the information accurately)
- *Analysis* (taking the information beyond the obvious)
- *Synthesis* (integrating the information in a way that is new or unique)

Be sure to state the purpose of a homework assignment. More students are likely to do it when they understand its purpose.

Some students, however, may well be able to adequately demonstrate knowledge, application, analysis, and synthesis without doing homework. All students should be evaluated on the basis of these outcomes,

~ FIGURE 3 ~

Questions for the Educator to Help Develop Academic Connection

1. Are there some teachers that you had who might be surprised by how well you have done in your life? What are some things you would want to say to them? What can you learn from them to help you be a better teacher?

2. Try to give your students a dream! Can you get them believing that they can succeed even when the odds are against them? As Steve Papesch (2000) suggests, hang a couple of signs in your room and reinforce:

> DO NOT BE AFRAID TO BE SMART
> YOU KNOW MORE THAN YOU THINK

3. Do you create excitement and challenge that students do not want to miss?

4. Do you allow students to explore and build on the material?

5. Are you excited to know that not all of your students learn and act exactly the same and that what works for one may not work for another?

6. What can you do to promote learning that a computer can't?

rather than the process they used to get there. As such, it is advisable to make homework "optional." To encourage students to do homework, allow them to earn bonus points for successfully completed homework. These points can serve as a bank from which the students can draw to improve their grades when necessary.

Help your students relax. A growing body of research has shown that high anxiety affects learning and often leads to symptoms associated with attention-deficit hyperactivity disorder (ADHD). Further, relaxation training can lead to a decrease in tension and in some of the primary symptoms associated with ADHD (Garber, Garber, & Spizman, 1996). Many studies have suggested strategies for relaxation to increase learning (Curwin & Mendler, 1997; Mendler, 1991). Techniques such as progressive relaxation and variations of meditation can help students deal more effectively with stress and, therefore, improve their ability to learn.

Strategies for Developing Social Connection ~

Have a problems-and-solutions center. Students submit classroom or personal problems about which they would like advice, suggestions, or input from their peers. Issues of concern can be written and deposited in a shoebox, with students then invited to offer solutions. The author can share his name or submit anonymously (expect that most will be anonymously). The teacher is also welcome to use this as a vehicle. For example, if you notice or have heard about various forms of bullying or harassment, you can express your concerns and ask for student input.

Have a thank-you center or bulletin board. Students are invited to share written appreciations of each other. You can use 3" x 5" index cards or the computer. This is always a highly affirming experience. If you are so inclined, it can be fun to have a weekly drawing in which you place all "appreciated" index cards in a central place. You can ask students on a random basis to pull out one of the cards and read it to the class. The winner (student who was "appreciated") gets a gift certificate (fast food, movie tickets, etc.).

Play "Find someone who . . . " Many educators have built classroom connections with students by having them find other students who share the same hobbies, experiences, opinions, accomplishments, or characteristics as they. A sheet is prepared with the

title "Find Someone Who . . . " followed by questions that you believe might generate interest (see Figure 4). Students then must find others in the class who can answer each question satisfactorily. When a student finds someone who can answer the question, the respondent's initials are written next to that question. No question can be answered by more than one student, ensuring that each student will have to talk with several classmates.

Encourage the class to sponsor a charity event or fundraiser (such as collecting and distributing food donations for the local food bank). As mentioned in an earlier section, this is a great way to build social connection among your students.

~ FIGURE 4 ~

Find Someone Who . . .

1. . . . was born in the same month as you.

2. . . . wants to do the same kind of work as you after school.

3. . . . has struggled academically in the same subject as you.

4. . . . has a cat or dog for a pet.

5. . . . is the same astrological sign as you but born in a different month.

6. . . . hangs out with a different circle of friends than you.

7. . . . has made light of being ridiculed, even though it hurt their feelings.

8. . . . believes in gun control.

9. . . . thinks that things are better now than when your parents were kids.

10. . . . likes music as much as you do, but prefers a different style.

Use "think-pair-share." Allow for individual thinking time, followed by discussion with a partner, and then class discussion. Try to pair unlikely partners (those who appear to have little in common), who then report their findings to the group.

Ask for a summary to promote listening. Get in the habit of asking one student to summarize the information shared by another. For example, "Joe, please tell us what you heard Fred say and then offer your view about his findings."

Survey the class. Students feel involved when asked to share their opinions. One approach is to ask students about whether or not they agree with a certain point of view. Asking "How many people agree (or disagree) with _____ ?" can often start a lively discussion. Keep in mind that a genuine, wholehearted sharing of disagreements or differing points of view can build strong social connection, because it helps students fully understand and appreciate that there is more than one way to view an issue.

Acknowledge the benefits of "problem" behavior. Focusing on the positive aspects of problem behavior gives educators the chance to respond differently to students. It can help to reframe a negative behavior by exploring how such behavior actually benefits others. For example, students who interrupt others challenge our tolerance. A student who is tapping his pencil gives everyone else a chance to practice learning in the face of distraction. The class clown provides humor that can bring welcome relief to the intensity of learning.

Here's an interesting way you and the class might benefit from the behavior of students who refuse to do assignments. In a way, these students are "donating" the extra class time it might have taken them to do the work, to their classmates who have turned in their assignments. In addition, you have saved time by not arguing about whether the students are going to do the assignments. And you might gain time— and valuable increases in communication—in the long run if you can work out a "deal" with the "noncompliant" students.

As an educator, you might challenge yourself to consider actual benefits to yourself or the class that are attributable to problem behavior. This can open the door toward helping you and other students provide support to students in need by framing their problems as strengths worthy of notice.

Encourage students to help with each other's problems. Not all students have the same strengths, yet all can use their strengths to support each other when the classroom is viewed as a community. For example, students who "forget" to do their homework can be paired with a few who are encouraged to "remind" them to get their work done by giving a friendly phone call. When a student with a constant need for attention does goofy things to get noticed, share your concern with the class. For example, you could say, "Joe has a hard time settling down, and I think we can all help by forcing ourselves to pay attention to the lesson even though we know he can be funny." Some students will not bring required materials to class; encourage all students to "donate" supplies such as pencils and paper. Suggest that those who "borrow" supplies either replace or donate something that might benefit a classmate in the future.

Give students problem-solving tools. You and the students can build a stronger sense of classroom community when problem-solving becomes the norm. Don't let mounting problems interfere with teaching and learning; give your students tools to solve them. The following five-step process is a fairly simple way to teach problem-solving:

1. Define the problem specifically in terms of how it negatively affects either your ability to teach or the students' ability to learn.

2. Ask students to explore why they think this problem is occurring. You can simplify by first asking them "What is good about [the situation, or the behavior, or the incident]?" (Be specific.)

3. Ask students to consider what is bad about the situation, behavior, or incident: "How do you think this creates a problem?"

4. Invite and list possible solutions.

5. Evaluate solutions for advantages and disadvantages, selecting those with the greatest likelihood of actually solving the problem.

Let students make some of the rules. By the time students have reached high school, they have already been drilled on rules and consequences many times. You can encourage a sense of community by involving your students in the process of developing the rules for your classroom. First, introduce the things you value in a classroom and in school; for instance, all classrooms need to be safe, respectful places that value diversity. And all students need to feel sufficiently comfortable to ask questions without being worried about whether they will be humiliated by classmates (or their teacher).

It is best to establish these classroom values and then invite your students to develop specific rules that the class is expected to follow. Extensive information is available on developing effective classroom rules and consequences with input from students (Curwin & Mendler, 1988, 1997, 1999).

Agree to change any rule students resist, as long as they provide an acceptable alternative. Be sure to explain the purpose of all classroom rules and then offer to change any rule as long as the class can come up with an acceptable alternative that accomplishes the same thing. I remember providing consulting services to the Wildwood Alternative School, a day school for disruptive students who had been kicked out of their regular schools. Staff had initiated a "locked bathroom" policy because of numerous bathroom abuses best left to your imagination. If a student wanted to use the bathroom, he had to get permission and a key. He also had to sign in and out for accountability purposes. Naturally, the students complained bitterly about this and were continually nagging staff to change the policy. I proposed that the staff should let students know that the policy could be changed, provided the student council offered alternative methods to ensure that bathrooms were adequately maintained (such as students monitoring bathroom conditions and cleaning as needed). Staff offered this option to student leaders. The students never did offer an alternative, but they did stop griping! Had they agreed to form a "bathroom squad" without coercion (such as by lottery), and assume responsibility for sanitary maintenance, it would have been interesting to measure improvement.

Look for opportunities to get students involved in school matters. Most schools have student councils that become involved in a variety of school projects, but not all students feel connected to these groups. Look for as many ways as you can to get your students connected to school issues. Reach out to kids who seem disconnected and try to get them actively involved. Most school committees could benefit from student involvement. For example, some of the students who frequently break rules might be invited to join or serve as consultants to the school's discipline committee. Students who are frequently in conflict with others can be invited for training as school mediators. When students are empowered to handle responsibilities related to their own problems, the connection they experience often leads to changed behavior.

Figure 5 suggests questions to reflect on concerning social connections.

Encourage "complaint" letters. When your students complain about issues over which you have little to no control, redirect their energy by suggesting that they write a business letter to the source of their complaint. For example, if they gripe about a homework or dress-code policy developed by the school board, then the letter they write could be directed to the school board. Suggest that their letter needs to contain the specific problem, why they view it as a problem, and at least one proposed solution.

You can also direct students to the source of their complaint in other ways. For example, when students complain about a policy that prohibits wearing hats or caps in school, let them know who is responsible for the policy (such as the faculty council), when they meet, and how to be heard (by attending a meeting, sending a letter; or signing a petition). Not only does this help students build a social connection, it also teaches appropriate avenues for seeking change.

Have an "absence" communicator. A nice touch is to have students call each other after an absence.

~ FIGURE 5 ~

Questions for the Educator to Develop Social Connection

1. Do you spend time helping students get to know each other?

2. What specific activities would work for you to deepen the social connection among your students?

3. Do you encourage and allow their interests to become an integral part of the class?

4. Are you highlighting specific ways that students can get along with each other more peacefully and effectively?

5. When put-downs or other divisive comments are heard, do you set limits, and stop class to address the issue in a manner that gets students thinking and problem-solving?

6. Are there specific ways that exist at your school and in your classroom for all students, including those who are shy and who don't talk much, to express their concerns about themselves or fellow classmates?

Students can either volunteer for this job, or you can establish a rotating list. When a student is absent, the caller can express concern and share information about the lessons the student missed. It is best to have parents sign a permission slip that allows their phone number to be on the list. Another option is to use e-mail for the same purpose. (Again, permission is necessary to avoid invasion of privacy.)

Allow some time for "wouldn't it be great if"
reflections. When the energy in your class is low, awaken your students by having them brainstorm answers to the sentence: "Right now, wouldn't it be great if _____ ." Let them to be as serious or as unconventional as they would like.

Show them how to take a stand. Learning to be assertive in the face of unwelcome invitations or undesirable comments is an important life skill that we can help students acquire. Here are two good questions that can lead to conversations about how to handle difficult peer situations:

1. What have you heard or seen students say or do that makes you mad?

2. Why do you think people say or do these things?

Students will offer many answers to the first question. To the second question, it can help to say,

> If anybody said or did the things that make you mad, do you think they are trying to give you power or rob you of your power? If you wanted to maintain your own power, let's look together at how we might best handle these situations.

Foster a "learn to win" attitude. When it is apparent that one student is goading another, Allison Seielstad, a middle school educator in Buford, Tennessee, asks the student being bothered, "Is _____ saying this to make you angry or happy?"

Virtually always, the student answers, "Angry."

She next asks, "Are you angry?"

Usually the student responds, "Yes."

The next follow-up question is, "Are you giving him what he wants?" This helps help the student recognize that an angry, upset, irritated response is giving the antagonist the reaction he desires.

Seielstad then asks the student, "Then who is winning?" and concludes with "Whom do you want to win?" The goal is to teach students that a response that is neutral or doesn't show anger allows the victimized student to "win." Students are told, "Learn to win," which becomes the cue whenever one student starts in on another.

Hold occasional class meetings. Involve students on a regular basis to discuss whatever issues of importance and relevance affect them. All feedback and opinions are allowed during discussion. The only requirements are that no putdowns are allowed and that students are not allowed to talk about other students who are not present.

Break bread together. There is no more powerful way to build rapport with adolescents than to eat with them. You might plan a meal featuring dishes from a country or culture being studied. You could also set aside one day each month or marking period when snacks are permissible and even encouraged in the classroom.

Have "relevant issues" time. Each week, you could devote a few minutes on a specific day to allow for open discussion of topics relevant to your students. You can initiate this discussion by bringing in an article or survey about a contemporary issue and asking your students to discuss their thoughts and opinions. For example, you can open by saying,

I read an article recently that I really want your thoughts about. It said that 80 percent of all students have cheated on school exams and that 50 percent think there is nothing wrong with doing this. Do you think this survey is right? What is there about our culture that makes so many young people think that cheating is okay?

Foster a "Secret Santa" exchange. This is such a fun practice that faculties often share this with each other during the holiday season to express goodwill and good wishes. It is worth extending this tradition of good cheer to students. "Secret Santa" is a fun opportunity to give and get appreciations from each other. Each student draws the name of another and becomes his or her "Secret Santa." During the holiday season, for one week, "Santa" offers daily messages of appreciation (in ways that do not involve money) to his or her recipient. At the end of the week, each student can guess who his or her Santa is.

Interrupt "language" before it escalates. Confront put-downs directly. Let your students know that you do not tolerate hurtful language or behavior. Give examples of put-downs that you have heard, and define limits regarding such language. Whenever someone steps over the line, confront the person in a consistent, firm, and low-key way. Students need to know that degrading language is the first step in the spiraling sequence that leads to harassment and violence. When someone steps over the boundary, firmly say, "We don't say that here. Thanks for your help."

Bury put-downs. Judy Black, a middle school teacher in Milwaukee, Wisconsin, has a creative way of decreasing the use of put-downs among her students. She explains that put-downs affect the way students think and feel about themselves and each other. Ms. Black tells her students that in the classroom, put-downs have no useful place. She then has students say and write down all the put-downs that they have ever used or heard. Each put-down is written on a slip of paper and placed into a shoebox. After the slips have been collected, the class goes outside and conducts a formal burial of the shoebox with the put-downs inside. From that moment forward, any put-down that has been buried can no longer be used. Periodic reburial ceremonies are conduced for put-downs that are initially missed.

Deal with disrespectful behavior even when it involves students who are not in your class. Many educators are understandably uncomfortable confronting inappropriate student behavior when it comes from an unknown student in a public setting, such as the hallway or cafeteria. Many educators would rather ignore the situation and walk away, rather than deal with an unfamiliar student in an unpredictable situation. Unfortunately, nothing contributes to students' fear factor more than watching faculty walk away from such an incident. Use the following sequence to confront the offending student in a safe and effective manner—and perhaps build a positive relationship with the student:

1. Say "Good morning" in a friendly way.

2. Tell the student, "I know you didn't mean anything by [describe the student's objectionable behavior], but the school rule is _____ ."

3. Expect cooperation: "Thanks for your help."

4. Offer future support: "Let me know if there's ever anything I can do to help you."

5. Conclude: "See you around [say student's name, or ask for his or her name]." Extend your hand for a handshake.

Start a suggestion box. This is a respectful way of soliciting suggestions for improvement from your students. Tell them that you are always eager to make the class a better place for them and that you welcome any idea that they think will improve the learning atmosphere. Explain that anybody who has a suggestion should write it up and place it in the "Suggestion Box." Let students know that you read all suggestions and that you will either do what is suggested or you will explain to the student who made the suggestion your reasoning for not doing it. Tell them that if they want feedback on their suggestions, they must sign their names. Otherwise, you are under no obligation to respond to the suggestion.

A variation of this is to have a "feedback box" in which students can offer input and suggestions for improvement to you or each other. Appreciations can also be offered. You can let them know that feedback that contains put-downs or unacceptable language or that relates to a student who is absent will not be shared. Set aside a regular time to share "feedback" with the class.

Create safe, visible ways for students to express their concerns. Students need to know that their input is not only valued, but is essential to keep the school a safe, caring place. In virtually all cases of deadly school violence, the disconnected, alienated students have shared their intentions with fellow students. We need to clearly convey to our students that whenever they hear a threat of violence from a classmate, or are aware of a potentially life-threatening issue such as suicide or an eating disorder, they must share this information with an adult.

They can share directly or indirectly. Indirect means of sharing could include an anonymous tip line or "concern" boxes stationed in such places as the main office, the counseling center, or with the school nurse. Concerned students could either write up the issue themselves, or the school could provide a simple form to fill out. The form could contain just a few simple sentences to be filled in:

Thank you for taking a moment to keep our school safe and to show concern for a fellow student. Please answer the following:

I'm concerned about _____

[name of the student].

Specific things I have heard, seen, or been told
by others that make me concerned are

_____.

Your name _____ (optional)

Teach the use of "I" messages. When you need to
give feedback that conveys either approval or disap-
proval, using an "I" message lessens the likelihood that a
student will be defensive. Teach students to use straight-
forward "I" messages to share their thoughts and feelings, as well. The feedback is given in three parts:

1. Tell the student what he or she
did ("When you   " [for example,
"use putdowns"]).

2. Tell how it affects you or others
positively or negatively ("I [we] **feel [get, am]** . . ."
[for example, "get distracted, as do others"]).

3. Tell what you want, need, or expect (for example, "so your cooperation beginning right now is
much appreciated").

More information about "I" messages can be found
elsewhere (Curwin & Mendler, 1988, 1999; Mendler,
1991).

For the Administrator ~

Too often, rifts between educators prevent them from providing the support necessary to help students achieve the many worthwhile goals set before them. Teachers often feel criticized and unsupported by administrators. Administrators, meanwhile, often feel caught in the middle of unending conflicts, and in attempting to please everybody, rarely succeed in pleasing anybody. This friction can trickle down throughout the school system, and eventually end up negatively affecting the students.

Students will learn better and feel safer when they can trust that the people in charge care about them. The principal, other administrators, office staff, and teacher leaders must continually realize that they set the tone. Whether or not people travel the extra mile often depends on how supported they feel. Busy teachers are more likely to reach out to their students when they are recognized and feel cared for by their administrators.

Occasionally, administrators must make accommodating changes within the school structure. For example, an increasing numbers of high schools and middle schools begin school with a short advisory period. During this time, a limited number of students are assigned to an educator, who provides interaction and mentoring. The goal is for educators to help students start the day in a positive way, provide advice, and occasionally hold parent conferences. Students are usually advised by the same educator/advisor throughout their entire tenure at the school.

There are many ongoing policies and activities (usually minor) that can make the difference. As an administrator or teacher leader, be a model of what you expect. If you want to encourage teachers to greet students, then be out in the hall greeting staff in a friendly manner as they arrive. Send notes of appreciation to staff when you notice their efforts. My wife's principal encourages his staff to write comments of appreciation about each other. These are read at staff meetings. My wife beamed when she came home after a faculty meeting during which another staff member shared an appreciation about her.

Work at creating a climate of cooperation and sharing among your staff. A high school teacher recently described how each department in his school has a bulletin board in the office. One side is labeled "FOR SALE," and the other is labeled "HELP WANTED." Under "HELP WANTED," faculty are

encouraged to leave a note asking for possible strategies when they are stumped by a student, class, or
issue. The "FOR SALE" side lists specific suggestions or
strategies designed to help address the problem and
that have been successful in the past.

Direct, hands-on support for staff can be expressed
by not sending students back to class immediately
after they have been referred for disciplinary action.
Read between the lines and recognize the exasperation that leads to an office referral. In most cases, a
truly honest referral written by a teacher would read,
"One of us had to leave, and it was either going to be
the student or me. Since the contract says I have to
stay, I am sending you the student."

When criticism is necessary, take the time to
explore how you might be able to help staff achieve
the necessary expectations. Ask before you judge. A
second-year teacher concerned about pleasing her
administrator explained how upset she became when
she was criticized for ignoring an unruly student's

behavior while being observed. A closer look found
that the student in question had a history of explo-
siveness; and the teacher and mental health staff
members had crafted a behavior plan that mapped
out when to ignore the student and when to inter-
vene. Rather than presenting written criticism, the
administrator could have expressed concern and
asked for an explanation while offering assistance,
such as,

> I noticed that you seemed to ignore Bob's inap-
> propriate behavior, and I am concerned that he
> and other students may be getting the wrong
> message. I have some ideas that I think might
> work better, but before I share them, can you
> help me understand your thinking about him?

When teachers know they can count on at least some
visible support when they are stressed, they are more
likely to open their minds and hearts to challenging,
difficult students.

Important administrative support can also be
expressed by helping each teacher feel safe and confident in the event of crisis. Administrators should
work with teachers to develop a classroom crisis plan
specifying how to handle chaotic situations such as

fistfights, tossed furniture, and thrown objects. The plan should include what actions the teacher should take, what the students should do, and how to get help when needed. Administrators need to take the lead in developing practices that keep the school safe. This includes having a school safety plan complete with preventive measures, such as a tip hotline and the monitoring of either spoken or written concerns from students and staff. A threat assessment team needs to be trained and available at a moment's notice to address any concerns that have been expressed.

Finally, use school policy to provide guidelines, but value people more than the policy. We can set an example for the community. For example, I recently encountered a mind-numbing series of policies, procedures, and bureaucratic rules when I switched long-distance telephone companies and was mistakenly charged for two switching fees rather than one. The extra charge was only $10, but I pursued a refund vigorously through a forest of voicemail and layers of supervisors and managers at two companies. Exasperated at the rigidity I encountered at every turn, I finally hung up after an hour of frustration, still out the $10. After this incident, I was grateful for my well-learned sense of morality that prohibits me from initiating physical harm toward others.

To keep our schools safe, we must work hard to keep from acquiring bureaucratic rigidity. For example, when considering the consequences of misbehavior, have the courage to take the action that is most likely to teach a student better behavior, rather than one that may appear more "pleasing" to a complaining parent or more "punishing" to an angry teacher. Sadly, we live in an era when being politically correct is too often valued more than being educationally sound. Decisions are increasingly based more on what the student *has* rather than who the student *is*. Excusing or minimizing the heroic football quarterback's incursions is no more justified than failing to impose necessary consequences on a student who is labeled emotionally disturbed.

Numerous examples abound of school-based decisions that focus on concerns about potential parental or legal threats, rather than on sound educational policy. Nothing destroys confidence and trust more than yielding to such intimidation. Policies should be built to serve people, not the other way around. When parents (or anyone else) demand a certain action, the only concern of the administration should be how that action is likely to affect teaching and learning. In a school, policies that nurture teaching and learning need to be supported and enforced. Other policies need to be reviewed and either revised or eliminated. We must strive to make common sense, courtesy, and the purpose served by the policy more important than the policy itself.

Conclusion ~

These are difficult times for educators. Outside factors put a lot of pressure on teachers, such as high-stakes testing, preoccupied or uninvolved parents, unsavory media influences that promote sex and violence as solutions to life's problems, and a high-tech world that nourishes an expectation of immediate gratification. Yet children need what they have always needed—except that more children aren't getting what families and tightly knit communities once provided: connections to caring adults who love, challenge, and support them.

As educators, we have opportunities every day to touch, shape, and affect young lives for the better. With challenging students, the road is often bumpy and uncertain, with sudden turns, detours, and unexpected obstacles that make the trip an unending adventure, at once frustrating and exciting. It is often the small moments of interaction that matter most: smiling at a child, winking approval, sharing encouraging words when things aren't going well; firmly, consistently, and gently correcting behavior when needed. It is wise for us to be guided by the fact that ultimately it will not matter how many beautiful cars or homes we owned or rounds of golf we played, but touching the lives of children will.

It is my hope that this book provides you with strategies to help you persevere, and also reminds you that your genuinely optimistic attitude can instill the hope that a better life is achievable for every student.

•   •   •

At a retirement dinner that I attended recently for a master teacher, Linda Steinberg, who is also my good friend, Linda summarized the meaning of her 32-year teaching career by reading the following poem:

Success

To laugh often and much;

To win the respect of intelligent people and the
affection of children;

To earn the appreciation of honest critics and to
endure the betrayal of false friends;

To appreciate beauty;

To find the best in others;

To leave the world a bit better

Whether by a healthy child, a garden patch or a
redeemed social condition;

To know even one life has breathed easier because
you have lived.

This is to have succeeded.

—Adapted from a poem by Bessie A. Stanley

Note: This poem, often erroneously attributed to Ralph Waldo
Emerson, is available on many Web sites. See the Ralph Waldo
Emerson Home Page for a discussion (http://www.rwe.org/pages/
how_to_cite.htm).

References and Bibliography ~

Brendtro, L. K., Brokenleg, M., & Van Bockern, S. (1990). *Reclaiming youth at risk*. Bloomington, IN: National Educational Service.

Canfield, J., Hansen, M. V., & Kirberger, K. (Eds.). (1997). *Chicken soup for the teenage soul: 101 stories of life, love and learning* (Chicken Soup for the Soul Series). New York: Health Communications.

Cousins, N. (1980). *Anatomy of an illness*. New York: W. W. Norton.

Covey, S. (1989). *The seven habits of highly successful people*. New York: Simon & Schuster.

Curwin, R., & Mendler, A. (1988). *Discipline with dignity*. Alexandria, VA: Association for Supervision and Curriculum Development.

Curwin, R., & Mendler, A. (1997). *As tough as necessary*. Alexandria, VA: Association for Supervision and Curriculum Development.

Curwin, R., & Mendler, A. (1999). *Discipline with dignity* (rev. ed.). Alexandria, VA: Association for Supervision and Curriculum Development.

Dwyer, K., & Skiba, R. (1999). School violence: Listening to the students. *NASP Communique, 28*(2), 4. (Published by the National Association of School Psychologists). [Online article]. Available: http://www.nasponline.org/publications/cq282violence.html

Garber, S. W., Garber, M. D., & Spizman, R. F. (1996). *Beyond Ritalin*. New York: Random House.

Garbarino, J. (1999, December 20). Some kids are orchids. *Time*, p. 51. [Online article]. Available: http://www.time.com/time/magazine/article/0,9171,1101991220-35858,00.html

Glasser, W. (1990). *The quality school*. New York: Harper & Row.

Karvalas, K. (Ed.). (1998). *The best of success: Quotations to illuminate the journey of success* (Series). Franklin Lakes, NJ: Career Press.

Maslow, A. H. (1971). *The farther reaches of human nature*. New York: Viking.

Mendler, A. (1991). *Smiling at yourself: Educating young children about stress and self-esteem*. Santa Cruz, CA: ETR Associates.

Mendler, A. (1992). *What do I do when . . . How to achieve discipline with dignity in the classroom*. Bloomington, IN: National Educational Service.

Mendler, A. (1997). *Power struggles: Successful techniques for educators*. Rochester, NY: Discipline Associates.

Mendler, A., & Curwin, R. (1999). *Discipline with dignity for challenging youth*. Bloomington, IN: National Educational Service.

Papesch, S. (2000). Insights on teaching from the job. *Education Digest, 65*(7), 32.

Rose, M. (2000, February). High schools that soar: Discovering what works in school-to-career programs. [Online article].

American Teacher, 84(5), 10–11, 19. Available: http://www.aft.
org/publications/american_teacher/feb00/soar2.html

Rosenthal, R., & Jacobson, L. (1968). *Pygmalion in the classroom.*
Fort Worth, TX: Holt, Rinehart and Winston.

Rutter, M. J. (1990). Psychosocial resilience and protective mecha-
nisms. In J. Rolf (Ed.), *Risk and protective factors in the development of psychopathology* (pp. 181–214). New York: Cambridge
University Press.

Schneider, B., & Stevenson, D. (1999). *The ambitious generation:
America's teenagers, motivated but directionless.* New Haven, CT:
Yale University Press.

Seita, J., Mitchell, M., & Tobin, C. (1996). *In whose best interest?
One child's odyssey, a nation's responsibility.* Elizabethtown, PA:
Continental Press.

U.S. Secret Service. (2000, October). *Safe school initiative: An
interim report on the prevention of targeted violence in schools.*
Washington, DC: National Threat Assessment Center, U.S.
Secret Service.

Werner, E., & Smith, R. (1992). *Overcoming the odds: High-risk children from birth to adulthood.* Ithaca, NY: Cornell University
Press.

About the Author ~

Allen N. Mendler, Ph.D., is a school psychologist, parent, teacher, educational consultant, and seminar leader based in Rochester, New York.

He has worked extensively with children of all ages in both general and special education settings. Mendler's emphasis is on developing effective frameworks and strategies for educators and youth professionals to help difficult students succeed. As one of the internationally acclaimed authors of *Discipline with Dignity* (ASCD, rev. ed., 1999), Mendler has given thousands of workshops and is highly acclaimed as a motivational speaker and trainer for several educational organizations. He was presented with the Crazy Horse Award in 1995 for courage in reaching disadvantaged youth. Mendler is the author or coauthor of several books, including *As Tough as Necessary: Countering Violence, Aggression, and Hostility in Our Schools* (ASCD, 1997), *What Do I Do When . . . ? How to Achieve Discipline with Dignity in the Classroom,* and *Power Struggles: Successful Techniques for Educators.* His articles have appeared in many journals, including *Educational Leadership, Phi Delta Kappan, Reclaiming Children and Youth,* and *Reaching Today's Youth.*

Contact the author at Discipline Associates, P.O. Box 20481, Rochester, NY 14602. Home and fax: 716-427-2659; office 800-772-5227; e-mail: allenmendler@rocketmail.com

For online excerpts of this book and of *Discipline with Dignity* and *As Tough as Necessary,* visit the ASCD Web site (www.ascd.org), click on the Reading Room, then enter "Mendler" in the search screen.

Related ASCD Resources: Classroom Management— Connecting with Students

ASCD stock numbers are noted in parentheses.

Audiotapes

Brain Research Applied to Classroom Management by Gene Van Tassell (#200126)

Changing the Ways Teachers and Students Think About and Respond to Classroom Management by H. Jerome Freiberg, Armandina Farias, Silvia McClure, and Wanda Watson (#296180)

Effective Discipline: Getting Beyond Rewards and Punishments by Marvin Marshall (#297190)

Student Discipline in Democratic Classrooms by Antwanette Hill and H. Jerome Freiberg (#297054)

Print Products

As Tough as Necessary: Countering Violence, Aggression, and Hostility in Our Schools by Richard L. Curwin and Allen N. Mendler (#197017)

Beyond Discipline: From Compliance to Community by Alfie Kohn (#196075)

Classroom Management by Robert Hanson (ASCD Professional Inquiry Kit #998059)

Classroom Management/Positive School Climate (ASCD Topic Pack #198219)

Connecting Character to Conduct: Helping Students Do the Right Things by Rita Stein, Roberta Richin, Richard Banyon, Francine Banyon, and Marc Stein (#100209)

Discipline with Dignity (2nd ed.) by Richard L. Curwin and Allen N. Mendler (#199235)

Managing to Teach: A Guide to Classroom Management (2nd ed.) by Carol Cummings (#300268)

Power Struggles: Successful Techniques for Educators by Allen N. Mendler (#301233)

Talk It Out: Conflict Resolution in the Elementary Classroom by Barbara Porro (#196018)

Winning Strategies for Classroom Management by Carol Cummings (#100052)

Videotapes

Catch Them Being Good: Reinforcement in the Classroom, featuring Pat Wolfe (3-tape series #614162)

Managing Today's Classroom (3-tape series #498027)

For additional resources, visit us on the World Wide Web (http://www.ascd.org), send an e-mail message to member@ascd.org, call the ASCD Service Center (1-800-933-ASCD or 703-578-9600, then press 2), send a fax to 703-575-5400, or write to Information Services, ASCD, 1703 N. Beauregard St., Alexandria, VA 22311-1714 USA.